THE SECOND BOOK OF GENERAL IGNORANCE

John Lloyd is a broadcaster by trade. As a radio producer he devised *The News Quiz* and *To the Manor Born* before moving to television to start *Not the Nine O'Clock News*, *Spitting Image* and *Blackadder*. He lives by the motto of the German mystic Henry Suso (1300–66): 'By ignorance the truth is known.'

John Mitchinson is from the world of books. The original Marketing Director of Waterstone's, he became Managing Director of Cassell, where he published The Beatles, Michael Palin and *Brewer's Dictionary of Phrase and Fable*. He's with the Chinese philosopher Lao-Tzu: 'To know that you do not know is the best. To pretend to know when you do not know is a disease.'

Visit us at www.qi.com or follow us on
www.twitter.com/qikipedia

D1341377